INFOMOJIS

NATURAL DISASTERS

WAYLAND
www.waylandbooks.co.uk

First published in Great Britain
in 2018 by Wayland
Copyright © Hodder and Stoughton, 2018
All rights reserved

Editor: Amy Pimperton
Produced by Tall Tree Ltd
Editor: Jon Richards
Designer: Ed Simkins

ISBN: 978 1 5263 0697 5

Wayland
An imprint of Hachette Children's Group
Part of Hodder and Stoughton
Carmelite House
50 Victoria Embankment
London EC4Y 0DZ

An Hachette UK Company
www.hachette.co.uk
www.hachettechildrens.co.uk

Printed and bound in China

MIX
Paper from
responsible sources
FSC® C104740
www.fsc.org

This book uses different units to measure different things:

Distance is measured in metres (m) and kilometres (km).

Area is measured in square kilometres (square km).

Volume is measured using cubic kilometres (cubic km).

Temperature is measured in degrees Celsius (°C).

Speed is measured using kilometres per hour (kph).

Mass is measured using megatonnes (1 million tonnes) and gigatonnes (1 billion tonnes).

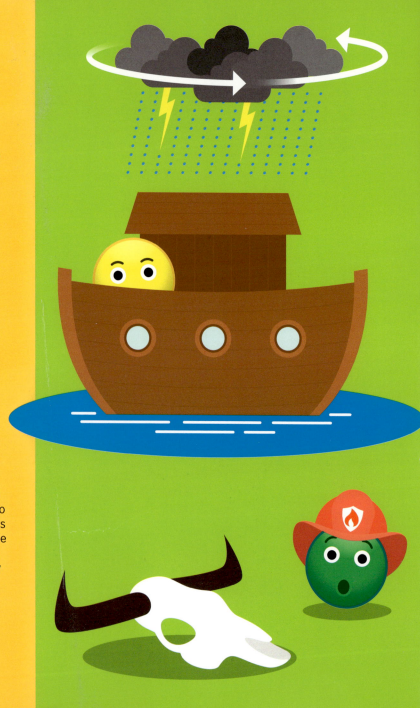

WHAT ARE NATURAL DISASTERS? 4

EARTHQUAKES 6

TSUNAMIS 8

VOLCANOES 10

AVALANCHES AND LANDSLIDES 12

TROPICAL CYCLONES 14

THUNDERSTORMS AND HAILSTORMS.. 16

TORNADOES 18

BLIZZARDS 20

FLOODS 22

DROUGHTS 24

FOREST AND BUSH FIRES 26

DISASTERS FROM SPACE 28

GLOSSARY 30

INDEX 32

WHAT ARE NATURAL DISASTERS?

Mountains explode, rivers burst their banks, the ground shakes, storms pummel the ground, enormous waves slam into coasts and pieces of rock fall from space! Sometimes, planet Earth can be a dangerous place to live!

Q: What is a natural disaster?

A: It is a naturally occurring event that causes a lot of damage and may kill a lot of people.

According to the Utah Avalanche Center, in the USA, in 90 per cent of avalanche deaths, the fall of snow was caused by the weight of the victim or someone else with them.

More than 1,000 earthquakes occur each day, but many are too small to notice. Earthquakes most commonly occur where two of Earth's tectonic plates meet. The movement of these plates releases huge amounts of energy, causing the ground to shake.

AVALANCHE

The slipping of rocks, soil and mud down the side of a mountain are known as landslides. They can cause huge amounts of damage if they occur close to a built-up area.

The huge torrent of water that creates a flood can have many causes, including unexpected rainfall, tidal surges from the sea, the failure of a dam, or it could be a result of regular seasonal conditions.

Warm tropical seas are the breeding grounds for powerful storms. When these hurricanes, typhoons and cyclones hit land, they can cause devastating damage.

When red-hot liquid rock bursts onto Earth's surface, the powerful volcanic eruptions can release rivers of lava, scorching clouds of gas and dust and explosive volcanic bombs.

The incredible power of a tornado, or twister, can carve a band of destruction across the land as it moves.

Triggered by underwater eruptions and earthquakes, tsunamis are huge walls of water that destroy coastal areas as they rush inland.

Volcanic bomb

TSUNAMI

←······ **Gas and dust**

Lava

Nature's most deadly
In the last 100 years, floods and drought have been responsible for 94 per cent of all deaths caused by extreme weather events.

While fast-moving fires can destroy huge areas of countryside and property, they can have positive effects, such as removing dead plants so that others can grow.

EARTHQUAKES

When the ground starts shaking, you know that there are some powerful forces at work. The swirling and churning of super-hot liquid rock deep beneath the ground slams chunks of Earth's crust into each other with devastating effects.

Shifting plates
When Earth's tectonic plates slide past each other, they can catch and get stuck. Energy builds up until the plates suddenly slip, releasing huge amounts of energy as a terrifying earthquake.

Epicentre – the point on the surface directly above the focus

Tectonic plate

Focus – the point where the earthquake occurs

Tectonic plate

My name is Charles Richter (1900–1985) and in 1935, I developed a scale for measuring the strength – or magnitude – of earthquakes, known as the Richter Scale (and named after me!).

CHARLES RICHTER

RICHTER SCALE MEASUREMENTS

1.0–1.9
Not felt or rarely felt (several million a year)

2.0–2.9
Felt by few people, no damage to buildings (more than one million a year)

3.0–3.9
Shakes indoor objects and usually felt by people in the affected area (more than 100,000 a year)

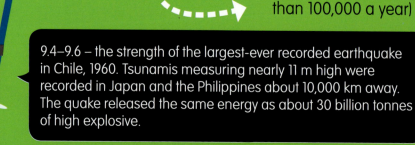

9.4–9.6 – the strength of the largest-ever recorded earthquake in Chile, 1960. Tsunamis measuring nearly 11 m high were recorded in Japan and the Philippines about 10,000 km away. The quake released the same energy as about 30 billion tonnes of high explosive.

The 2011 earthquake off the coast of Japan had a magnitude of 9.0–9.1 and was so powerful it moved parts of the entire country by almost 4 m. It caused such as shift in landmass that scientists calculate it sped up the rotation of Earth, shortening the length of a day by about 1.8 millionths of a second!

Whole lotta shakin' going on!

9.0+
Total destruction and permanent changes to ground features (one every 10–50 years)

Ouch!!! That hurt!

8.0–8.9
Severe damage and destruction with effects felt far away (one a year)

7.0–7.9
Damages most buildings and can cause damage up to 250 km from the epicentre (10–20 a year)

In January 1556, a massive earthquake in Shaanxi, China, with an estimated power of 8.0 on the Richter Scale cost the lives of up to 830,000 people, making it the deadliest ever.

4.0–4.9
Felt by most people in the affected area and causes minimal damage (10,000–15,000 a year)

5.0–5.9
Felt by everyone near the epicentre and can cause some damage (1,000–1,500 a year)

6.0–6.9
Moderate levels of damage and can be felt hundreds of kilometres from the epicentre (100–150 a year)

TSUNAMIS

Move Earth's crust violently enough and it will trigger powerful and catastrophic waves known as tsunamis. These can race inland causing huge levels of destruction.

The 1964 Alaska earthquake created a tsunami that was 67 m tall. That's 20 per cent taller than Italy's Leaning Tower of Pisa (56.4 m).

Surf's up, dude!

How a tsunami is formed

1. A sudden movement in the sea floor from an earthquake or volcanic eruption displaces a huge amount of water.

2. Waves spread out from the site of the disturbance at speeds of up to 800 kph.

3. As the waves approach the coastline, they slow down but grow in height.

The tsunami triggered by the 2011 earthquake off Japan (see page 7) created a tsunami that was almost 39 m high when it hit parts of the country. It flooded more than 560 square km. In total, the earthquake and tsunami caused an estimated US$235 billion of damage, more than any other in history.

It also led to meltdowns in three nuclear reactors at the Fukushima Daiichi Nuclear Power Plant.

— 2004 earthquake, Indonesia
— 2011 earthquake, Japan

Japan
Indonesia
Pacific Ocean
South Africa
Indian Ocean

On 26 December 2004, a powerful earthquake measuring 9.1–9.3 on the Richter Scale triggered a series of tsunamis that swept around the Indian Ocean. Waves up to 30 m high hit 14 countries, causing massive devastation and the deaths of up to 280,000 people. The tsunami was detected 8,500 km away in South Africa where a 1.5-m surge wave hit the shore 16 hours after the earthquake.

4. The waves slam into the shoreline causing huge levels of destruction.

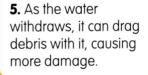

5. As the water withdraws, it can drag debris with it, causing more damage.

VOLCANOES

As well as causing powerful earthquakes, movements of Earth's crust can push red-hot liquid rock up to the surface causing violent volcanic eruptions.

1,250°C is the average temperature of lava.

90%
– the percentage of the world's volcanoes found around the Pacific Ocean, in a region known as the Ring of Fire.

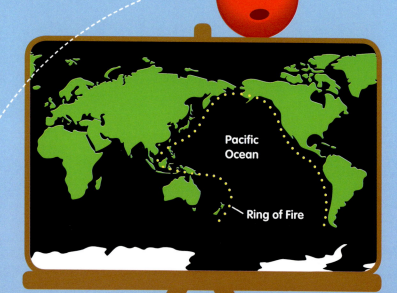

Pacific Ocean

Ring of Fire

Lava

1,900 – the number of volcanoes that are classed as active.

Active volcano – one that is erupting or erupts regularly.

Dormant volcano – one that has erupted recently and is now quiet, but could erupt again.

Fourpeaked Volcano in Alaska, USA, was thought to be extinct, until it erupted in 2006.

Extinct volcano – one that hasn't erupted for a long time and is unlikely to erupt again.

Volcano types

Composite – steep-sided cone made up of layers of ash and lava.

Shield – Gentle slopes made up of layers of lava

Cinder cone – Steep cone made from layers of ash, cinders and rock debris.

Q: What was the most powerful eruption ever recorded?

A: The most powerful eruption occurred on 27 August 1883, when the volcano on Krakatoa, now Indonesia, exploded. The force destroyed more than 70 per cent of the island and created an explosion equivalent to 200 megatonnes of TNT – four times more powerful than the strongest nuclear bomb ever exploded.

Cough! Cough!

In 1991, the eruption of Mount Pinatubo in the Philippines threw out 10 cubic km of lava and dust as well as 20 million tonnes of sulphur dioxide into the atmosphere. Scientists believe that the gases released caused temperatures around the world to drop by 0.5°C between 1991 and 1993.

AVALANCHES AND LANDSLIDES

When the force of gravity gets too much, huge chunks of snow, ice, rock and mud can hurl themselves down a mountain slope with terrible consequences.

An avalanche is a fall of snow down the side of a mountain. They can be caused by: the sheer weight of snow; earthquakes and volcanic eruptions; layers of snow sliding over each other; or by human interference – sometimes deliberately.

To help prevent avalanches, snow-covered slopes can be groomed using large snowploughs to stop too much snow building up in some spots. Snow fences are also set up to prevent the snow slipping, or explosives can be used to trigger small avalanches before too much snow builds up.

Types of avalanche

Slab avalanche – caused by fresh, damp snow breaking away in slabs.

Powder snow avalanche – caused by fresh powder snow sliding off older snow.

Glacier avalanche – caused by chunks of ice breaking away from a glacier.

When rock or mud slides down a mountain slope, it is called a landslide, landslip or mudslide. It can be caused by: a build-up of water beneath the surface; erosion of the bottom of a slope; a lack of plants to stabilise the slope; water from melting glaciers; as well as earthquakes or volcanic eruptions.

Evidence of landslides has been detected on both Venus and Mars.

During the First World War (1914–1918), up to 80,000 Austro-Hungarian and Italian soldiers were killed by avalanches in the Alps, which had been triggered by artillery fire.

The Galtür Avalanche in Austria in 1999 saw a wall of snow up to 50 m high hit the town of Galtür at 290 kph, killing 31 people.

An earthquake in Nepal in 2015 triggered a massive avalanche that swept through the base camp of Mount Everest, killing at least 22 people.

TROPICAL CYCLONES

Hold onto your hats, as the strongest storms on Earth are about to rip through these pages, with some facts that will really blow your mind!

Q: What do you call a tropical cyclone?

A: Tropical cyclones are called different names in different parts of the world. In the Indian Ocean they are called cyclones, in the Western Pacific, they are typhoons and in the Eastern Pacific and Atlantic they are called hurricanes.

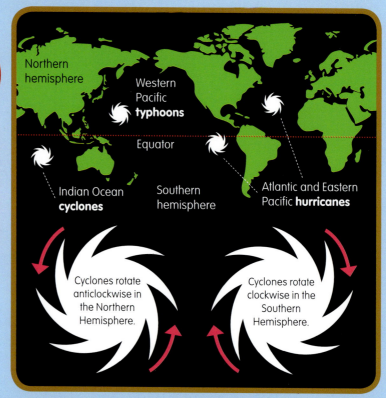

Northern hemisphere

Western Pacific **typhoons**

Equator

Indian Ocean **cyclones**

Southern hemisphere

Atlantic and Eastern Pacific **hurricanes**

Cyclones rotate anticlockwise in the Northern Hemisphere.

Cyclones rotate clockwise in the Southern Hemisphere.

How they form
Tropical cyclones form over the oceans in warm, tropical regions where temperatures reach 25°C for at least 50 m above the water surface.

1. Water vapour forms clouds that are pulled into tall columns by rising warm air, creating thunder clouds.

2. Rising air cools, becomes unstable and spreads out. The column starts to spin and winds reach 62 kph. This rotating thunderstorm is called a tropical depression.

Warm air   Warm air

3. When the winds reach 63 kph, the depression becomes a storm. The winds start to twist around the central eye of the storm.

Storm names
When a tropical storm forms it is given a name to make it easier to track and keep records. Storm names alternate between male and female names.

Costliest tropical cyclones
Hurricane Katrina in 2005 and Hurricane Harvey in 2017 both caused some US$125 billion worth of damage.

Deadliest storm
More than 500,000 people were killed by the Bholo cyclone when it hit East Pakistan (now Bangladesh) in November 1970.

USA

Typhoon Tip compared to the USA

Strongest winds
In April 1996, Cyclone Olivia produced gusts of wind that were recorded at 410 kph in Barrow Island, Australia.

Biggest storm
When it formed in October 1979, Typhoon Tip became the largest tropical cyclone ever recorded, measuring about 2,200 km across.

The eye of a tropical cyclone can be 50 km wide.

4. When winds reach 119 kph, the storm becomes a tropical cyclone. The cyclone increases its power as it moves over water before hitting land where it can cause immense damage.

THUNDERSTORMS AND HAILSTORMS

The flash of lighting and the crash of thunder tells you that a powerful storm is nearby. Get ready for torrents of water, the sparks from lighting bolts and maybe even hailstones falling from the sky!

How a thunderstorm forms

1. Warm air is forced upwards, where it cools and the water condenses, forming a towering cumulonimbus cloud, which can be 20 km high.

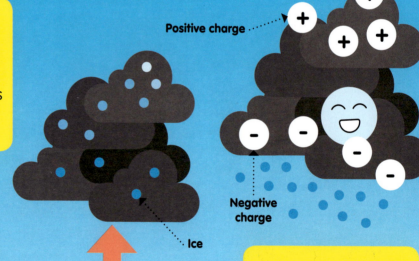

Positive charge

Negative charge

Ice

Warm air

2. As the warm air continues to rise, the larger water droplets freeze and fall. The falling ice rubs against rising droplets, picking up a negative electrical charge.

3. The negative charge collects at the bottom of the cloud, while the top of the cloud has a positive charge.

How hail forms

In the swirling wind currents of a thundercloud, droplets of water are churned up and down, freezing and joining together in layers to form hailstones. Winds of more than 180 kph can blow a hailstone up to a height of 10 km before it gets too heavy and falls.

The largest hailstone ever recorded fell on the town of Vivian, South Dakota, USA, on 23 July 2010. It measured 20 cm in diameter.

A lightning bolt has a temperature of about 30,000°C – about six times hotter than the surface of the Sun! This makes the air around the lightning very hot.

4. The negative charge is attracted to the ground, other clouds or objects, and when the attraction becomes too strong, a lightning bolt forms.

5. The super-hot air around the lightning bolt expands rapidly causing thunder.

In the USA, lightning kills 31 people on average every year.

TORNADOES

These enormous spinning funnels of air are so powerful that they can be some of the most destructive forces on the planet, throwing around everything in their path.

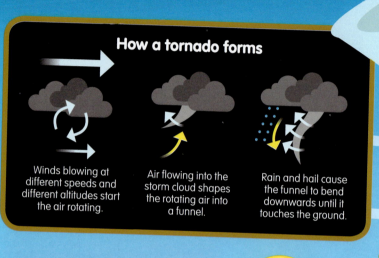

How a tornado forms

Winds blowing at different speeds and different altitudes start the air rotating.

Air flowing into the storm cloud shapes the rotating air into a funnel.

Rain and hail cause the funnel to bend downwards until it touches the ground.

Tornadoes can measure 3 km across and feature winds up to 480 kph. But they usually move at just 50 kph and only travel for about 10 km.

Q: Which country has the most tornadoes?

USA

Tornado Alley – the name given to an area of central USA that experiences a high number of tornadoes.

A: The USA has about 1,200 tornadoes every year, while Canada has less than 100, even though it's right next door!

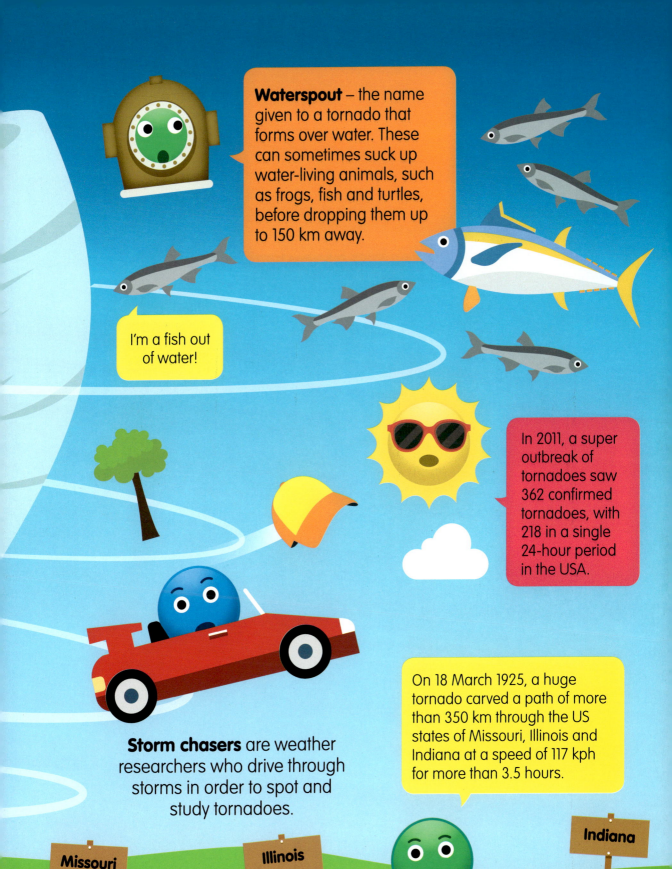

Waterspout – the name given to a tornado that forms over water. These can sometimes suck up water-living animals, such as frogs, fish and turtles, before dropping them up to 150 km away.

I'm a fish out of water!

In 2011, a super outbreak of tornadoes saw 362 confirmed tornadoes, with 218 in a single 24-hour period in the USA.

On 18 March 1925, a huge tornado carved a path of more than 350 km through the US states of Missouri, Illinois and Indiana at a speed of 117 kph for more than 3.5 hours.

Storm chasers are weather researchers who drive through storms in order to spot and study tornadoes.

Missouri

Illinois

Indiana

BLIZZARDS

While snow may look peaceful and pretty, combine it with strong winds and seriously cold conditions and you have the recipe for a terrible blizzard.

Q: When does a snowstorm become a blizzard?

A: A snowstorm becomes a blizzard when the wind blows stronger than 56 kph, reducing visibility to just 400 m.

Q: What was the Storm of the Century?

A: This powerful winter storm blew through North America in March 1993. At one point, it stretched from Canada down to Central America. It killed more than 300 people, caused more than US$2 billion of damage, and left more than 10 million homes without electricity.

In February and March 2008, a chain of snowstorms and blizzards hit much of China, including the country's large Taklamakan Desert. Here temperatures plunged to -32°C and the whole desert was covered in snow for the first time ever.

TAKLAMAKAN DESERT

Severe blizzards have winds faster than 72 kph with almost zero visibility and temperatures of less than -12°C.

A whiteout is a blizzard where downdrafts and heavy snow combine to create conditions where you can't tell the ground from the sky.

Blizzards in Antarctica are some of the most severe on the planet, with winds roaring at more than 160 kph.

Where are the snowiest cities on the planet?

Valdez, Alaska, USA
825 cm a year

Aomori City, Japan
760 cm a year

Sapporo, Japan
485 cm a year

Quebec City, Canada
380 cm a year

FLOODS

When water covers large areas of land, it can cause huge levels of damage by destroying crops and buildings and leaving thousands of people homeless.

Q: What can cause flooding?

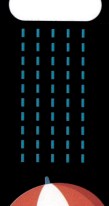

A: Excessive rainfall or snow supply water too quickly for it to run off or soak into the ground. Rivers burst their banks. Coastal floods are caused by storms, tsunamis or storm surges.

In 1931, a series of floods on the Yellow, Yangtze and Huai rivers in China caused one of the deadliest natural disasters ever recorded. Nearly 4 million people were killed by the floods that were caused by heavier than usual rain that year.

In 1530, a storm surge in the North Sea caused terrible flooding in the Netherlands, killing 100,000 people and washing away large parts of the regions of Flanders and Zeeland.

About 80 per cent of Bangladesh lies on a large flat area next to a river, known as a floodplain. Every year, melted water from glaciers high up in the Himalayas flows down the Ganges River. When this is combined with annual monsoon rains it causes devastating flooding. In 1998, about 75 per cent of the country was covered by water.

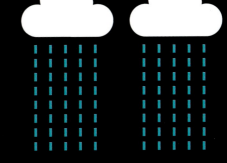

HIMALAYAS

Anyone got an umbrella?

Many religions, including Judaism, Christianity and Islam, contain stories of terrible floods.

Flood controls and defences include:

Flood barriers

Dams

River defences, such as weirs

Coastal defences, such as dykes and culverts

Built to protect London from excessive tidal floods, the Thames Barrier uses huge rotating metal gates that close to block the flow of water.

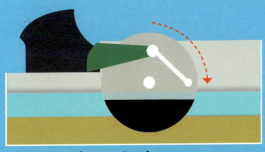

Thames Barrier open

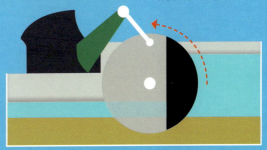

Thames Barrier closed

DROUGHTS

Most people enjoy a bit of warm weather, but when things get too hot, conditions can threaten health and lives. Prolonged periods of hot, dry weather can have devastating effects on the land and the people living there.

A **drought** is a long period with very little rainfall.

A **heatwave** is a long period of very warm weather.

Farming can be particularly affected by drought as, in many parts of the world, it uses more water than anything else. In California, for example, agriculture accounts for 80 per cent of the total water consumption.

The longest drought on record took place in Chile's Atacama Desert, which went without rain for 400 years.

ATACAMA DESERT

A drought between 1920 and 1921 in the Soviet Union lead to the deaths of nearly 5 million people.

HISTORICAL DROUGHTS

About 4,200 years ago, a 300-year-long drought may have led to the collapse of the Akkadians in Mesopotamia (modern Iraq), one of the world's first great civilisations.

A mega-drought lasting 60 years may have forced the Pueblo peoples to abandon Chaco Canyon, New Mexico, USA, in the 13th century.

In comparison, the worst drought in modern USA in the 1900s lasted just four years and was responsible for the Dust Bowl, when large areas of farmland in central USA turned to dust!

Causes of drought

- Lack of precipitation
- Extended dry season
- Effects of El Niño weather system
- Human activities, such as poor farming techniques
- Climate change

Normal year

El Niño year

El Niño
The variation in the temperature of the Southern Pacific Ocean can have disastrous effects on the weather and climate in countries right around the world. Large parts of South and Central America experience drier, hotter weather during an El Niño year, as well as southern and central Africa.

In July 2012, the US government declared natural disaster areas in 26 states across the country, making that drought the largest natural disaster in US history.

FOREST AND BUSH FIRES

Mix hot, dry weather, with the tinder-box conditions of scrub, bush or forests and you have the perfect recipe for a disastrous fire that can spread, well, like wildfire!

Fires can spread as fast as 11 kph in forests and up to 22 kph on grasslands.

Q: What are the main causes of bush fires?

In the right conditions, hot embers from fires can travel up to 20 km from the main site to cause new spot fires.

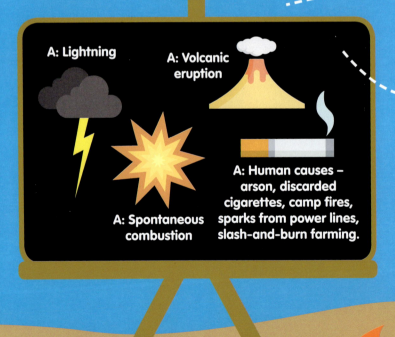

A: Lightning

A: Volcanic eruption

A: Spontaneous combustion

A: Human causes – arson, discarded cigarettes, camp fires, sparks from power lines, slash-and-burn farming.

1997 Indonesian forest fires

Caused by farmers practising slash-and-burn farming, these fires burnt an area of 80,000 square km – the same area as Lake Superior, the largest lake in North America.

Asia

Pacific Ocean

Malaysia

Singapore

Indonesia

Indian Ocean

Thick clouds of smoke and haze spread as far as Malaysia and Singapore.

While the fires are hazardous, the smoke can be even more deadly and estimates indicate that more than 300,000 people die from the effects of wildfire smoke every year.

The fires released up to 2.5 gigatonnes of carbon into the atmosphere, equivalent to nearly 40 per cent of the total amount released by the burning of fossil fuels each year.

Eucalyptus tree

Eucalyptus trees love bush fires. They produce highly flammable leaf litter and bark peelings, as well as the oil that seeps out of their bark. In some parts of Australia they are called 'gasoline trees'! Their seed pods open up when they are burnt, spreading the seeds onto soil that's rich in nutrients and free from other plant competition!

27

DISASTERS FROM SPACE

While everyday disasters usually come from the ground beneath our feet, the raging seas or the atmosphere, some of the deadliest forces come from the freezing vacuum of space.

Sun storms

The Sun throws out a constant stream of charged particles. Earth's magnetic field deflects these to the polar regions, where they are funnelled down to the atmosphere. Here, the charged particles interact with particles in the atmosphere to create glowing light displays called aurorae.

Every so often, the Sun throws out a much stronger burst of charged particles, which can have more damaging effects.

It can heat the atmosphere, causing it to expand. This can affect low-orbit satellites and, if they're not pushed into a new orbit, they can re-enter and burn up.

It can disrupt communications and navigation systems.

Shooting stars

As Earth moves around its orbit, it passes through the debris left by comets and asteroids. This debris burns up harmlessly to create meteors, or shooting stars. But some are big enough to hit Earth's surface. They are called meteorites.

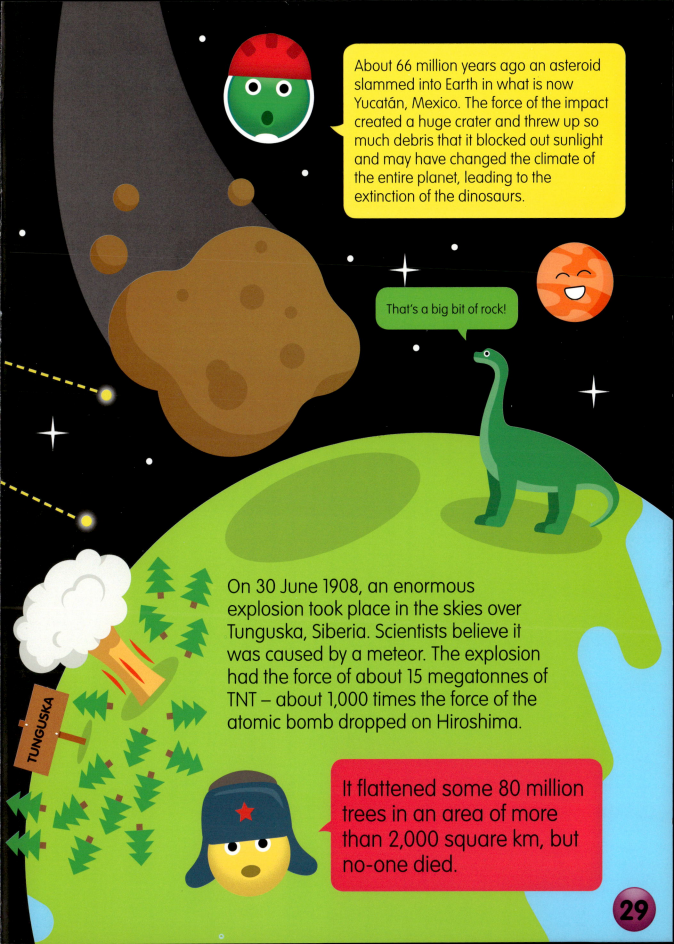

About 66 million years ago an asteroid slammed into Earth in what is now Yucatán, Mexico. The force of the impact created a huge crater and threw up so much debris that it blocked out sunlight and may have changed the climate of the entire planet, leading to the extinction of the dinosaurs.

That's a big bit of rock!

TUNGUSKA

On 30 June 1908, an enormous explosion took place in the skies over Tunguska, Siberia. Scientists believe it was caused by a meteor. The explosion had the force of about 15 megatonnes of TNT – about 1,000 times the force of the atomic bomb dropped on Hiroshima.

It flattened some 80 million trees in an area of more than 2,000 square km, but no-one died.

GLOSSARY

ACTIVE VOLCANO
This is a volcano that is erupting or erupts regularly.

ARTILLERY
Large land guns that are used by the military in warfare.

AURORAE
Bands of coloured light that occur high in the atmosphere. They are caused by the interaction of air molecules and charged particles from the Sun.

CHARGED PARTICLES
When an atom loses or gains an electron it becomes either positively or negatively charged. Charged particles are called ions.

CONDENSES
When a gas cools and turns into a liquid.

DUST BOWL
The name given to a time in the 1930s when a long drought destroyed large areas of farmland in the USA and Canada, and produced huge dust storms.

DYKE
A wall or channel that is built to prevent rivers or seawater from flooding an area of land.

EARTHQUAKE
The shaking of the ground caused by a sudden movement of Earth's tectonic plates or by a volcanic eruption.

EL NIÑO
A change in the normal temperature distribution in the Pacific Ocean, which can change the weather patterns across the whole world.

EPICENTRE
The place on Earth's surface directly above the site of an earthquake.

EROSION
When soil and rock are worn away by natural conditions, including wind, rain, rivers and glaciers.

FLOODPLAIN
A large flat area on either side of a river that is prone to flooding.

FOCUS
This is the point underground where an earthquake originates.

FOSSIL FUEL
Any type of fuel made from the remains of animals and plants that died a long time ago.

HURRICANE
The name given to a tropical cyclone that forms over the Atlantic or the Eastern Pacific. Hurricanes are powerful storms that form huge rotating spirals of cloud and can cause enormous amounts of damage when they hit land.

LANDSLIDE
A fall of rocks and earth down the side of a mountain.

LAVA
Molten rock that flows out of a volcano and over its surface.

METEOR
A piece of rock or metal that burns up in Earth's atmosphere.

NUCLEAR REACTOR
Where controlled nuclear reactions take place, which release energy and power a generator.

SLASH-AND-BURN FARMING
A farming method that involves clearing land by burning any trees and plants on it to make way for crops.

SNOWPLOUGH
A vehicle used to push snow to one side, usually to clear roads.

SULPHUR DIOXIDE
A gas with a sharp, unpleasant smell. It is created when sulphur within fuels burn, and can cause acid rain.

TECTONIC PLATES
The large slabs of rock that the Earth's crust has split into.

TIDAL SURGE
When high winds push the sea towards the coastline, creating a rise in sea levels and potential flooding.

TNT
An abbreviation of 'trinitrotoluene' – a very powerful, explosive substance.

TORNADO
A rotating storm that forms a funnel of violent winds. It is also called a twister.

TORNADO ALLEY
The name given to a part of North America where tornadoes most frequently occur.

TSUNAMI
A large wave caused by an underwater disturbance, such as an earthquake or a volcanic eruption.

VOLCANIC BOMB
A chunk of molten rock that is thrown out from a volcano. It then cools and solidifies before it hits the ground.

WHITEOUT
An event that occurs during a snowstorm or blizzard when visibility is so bad that you can't tell the difference between the ground and the sky.

INDEX

Alaska, USA 8, 10
Alps 13
Antarctica 21
asteroids 28, 29
Atacama Desert 24
aurorae 28
Australia 15, 25
Austria 13
avalanches 4, 12, 13

Bangladesh 15, 23
blizzards 20–21

Canada 18, 20, 21
Chile 6, 24
China 7, 20, 22
cyclones 5, 14, 15
Cyclone Olivia 15

droughts 5, 24–25

earthquakes 4, 6–7, 8,
    12, 13
El Niño 25
epicentre 6
eucalyptus trees 25
Everest, Mount 13

fires 5, 26–27
floods 5, 22–23
flood defences 23
Fourpeaked Volcano 10

Ganges River 23

hailstorms 17
heatwaves 24
Himalayas 23
Huai River 22
hurricanes 5, 14, 15
Hurricane Harvey 15
Hurricane Katrina 15

Indian Ocean 9
Indonesia 11, 25

Japan 6, 7, 9, 21

Krakatoa 11

landslides 4, 13
lava 5, 11, 12
lightning 16, 17, 26

Malaysia 25
Mars 13
meteorites 28
meteors 28, 29
Mexico 29

Nepal 13
Netherlands, The 22

Philippines 6, 11
Pinatubo, Mount 11

Richter, Charles 6
Richter Scale 6, 7
Ring of Fire 10

shooting stars 28
Singapore 25
snowploughs 12
South Africa 9
storm chasers 19
Sun 28

Taklamakan Desert 20
tectonic plates 4, 6
Thames Barrier 23
thunder 17
thunderstorms 16–17
tornadoes 5, 18–19
Tornado Alley 18
tropical cyclones 14–15
tsunamis 5, 6, 8–9, 22
Tunguska, Siberia 29
typhoons 5, 14, 15
Typhoon Tip 15

USA 17, 18, 19, 21, 25

Venus 13
volcanoes 5, 8, 10–11, 12,
    13, 26
volcanic bombs 5

waterspouts 19

Yangtze River 22
Yellow River 22